State Shapes Washington

Text copyright © 2008 by Black Dog & Leventhal Publishers, Inc.

Illustrations copyright © 2008 by Alfred Schrier

Published by
Black Dog & Leventhal Publishers, Inc.
151 W. 19th Street
New York, NY 10011

Distributed by
Workman Publishing Company
708 Broadway
New York, NY 10003

Manufactured in China

Cover and interior design by Sheila Hart

ISBN-13: 978-1-57912-775-6

h g f e d c

Library of Congress Cataloging-in-Publication Data

McHugh, Erin, 1952-
Washington / by Erin McHugh; illustrations by Alfred Schrier.
p. cm. -- (State shapes)

ISBN 978-1-57912-775-6
1. Washington (State)--Juvenile literature. I. Schrier, Alfred, ill. II. Title.

F891.3.M38 2008

979.7--dc22   2007039708

BY

ERIN MCHUGH

Illustrations by Alfred Schrier

BLACK DOG
& LEVENTHAL
PUBLISHERS
NEW YORK

Hi there! I'm George, and I'm going to show you tons of awesome stuff here in the Evergreen State. That's what we call the state of Washington. Hey, I really like your dog—what's her name?

Her name is Lily and I'm Mimi. Lily and I have traveled a long way to be here. This is the first time we've even seen the Pacific Ocean!

You can look, but you might not want to swim; the water's a lot colder than you'd think. In the summer, when it's hot outside, the water temperature here is often only 50°F. Washington is unique in many ways. We even have volcanoes!

No way! Do they ever explode?

You mean erupt, and yes, one did; it's called Mount St. Helens, and it wasn't that long ago either. I'll tell you more about it when we get there. In the meantime, I should tell you a little bit more about me. My full name is George Washington Bush, and I'm named after one of my ancestors.

6

Q. Who is pictured on the Washington state flag?

Wait a minute! George W. Bush?
Like the forty-third president of the United States?

Not exactly. My George W. Bush was an African-American man who came to Washington from Missouri in 1844; he was named after our first president, just like this state was. George Washington Bush was married to a white woman, which was very unusual in those days. In fact, in the southern United States, it was forbidden.

Why did they come way out here?

George had a friend who was a white man and they decided to travel west together. The Bushes had five kids by then, and they found that there was a lot of discrimination against them. They heard that Oregon, which is the state just south of here, had no laws discriminating against African Americans. But by the time they got there, the laws had changed. So they all crossed over the Columbia River, into what is now Washington, and settled in Tumwater, near Puget Sound. Native Americans and other explorers had visited here before George Washington Bush, but he's known as the state's founder.

 George Washington, of course! President Washington's head is set against a green background, which you might say is a shade of evergreen.

It's beautiful here, that's for sure.

Well, all the fir trees—which are also called coniferous trees—smell so good, and the air is fresh and clean. We only have approximately six million people in our whole state. To put that in perspective, New York City has more than eight million people! Back in 1850 when George Washington Bush was here, there were only 1,200 people in all of Washington.

My school has more kids than that!

Well, it wasn't an easy place to live back then. The weather can be pretty extreme in Washington. The highest temperature ever recorded here was 118°F. The funny thing is, it was recorded at a place called Ice Harbor Dam. The coldest day recorded was minus 48°F. And we once had sixty-four inches of snow in one day! It can also be really rainy in some parts of the state. The Cascades, which are the mountains that go from north to south all the way down to California, divide the state's weather. It's much colder in the eastern part of the state. To the west of the Cascades, the ocean air makes things wetter and milder.

Q. What are the names of all the volcanoes of the Cascade Mountains?

So what do you guys do for fun out here? Ski? Hike? Go camping? I'm confused!

We do it all! I'll bet you've never been white-water rafting. There are a lot of places to do that here. Skiing is popular too, and sailing, hiking, camping, biking, backpacking, and fishing, of course. We spend a lot of time outdoors! There's just about every kind of terrain, so you can do any kind of sport.

Yee-ha! This sounds like my kind of place. Are there some fun cities to visit too?

You bet. Let's start with a trip to the Pacific Ocean. Maybe we'll spot our state mammal, the orca whale. We can go whale watching.

 A. From north to south they are Mount Baker, Glacier Peak, Mount Rainier, Mount St. Helens, and Mount Adams.

9

Look at all the beaches!

This is Long Beach, which is perfectly named because it's the longest natural beach in the United States. There's some great stuff to eat in Washington too, especially from the ocean and rivers. Washington shellfish is famous, especially a bivalve that's called the geoduck. And you've got to pronounce it right: it sounds like *gooey-duck*.

I've never seen anything like this—it's huge!

Yup. We've got plenty of regular clams here, but geoducks run three to six pounds each! Washington has some of the best fishing you've ever seen. This is where everybody comes to catch sturgeon, salmon, halibut, crab, and tuna; it's a real fisherman's paradise.

Wait, what's all that, George? Up in the sky?

Q. What is the forty-ninth parallel?

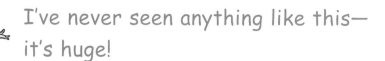

It's a bird, it's a plane, it's … the Washington State International Kite Festival, and is it fun! There are competitions and demonstrations, and people fly kites in formations: there's even a lighted night fly. Long Beach Peninsula is a swell place for kite flying—twenty-three miles of beach and lots of wind. The World Kite Museum and Hall of Fame is here, and it's the only kite museum on the continent. There are more than 1,500 kites on display that we can see.

Let's visit another little town called Pacific Beach; they like to say they're Washington's best-kept secret. They put on festivals all year long, but my favorite is the Kelpers Festival and Shake Rat Rendezvous on Labor Day weekend.

Kelper? Shake rat? What are you talking about, George?

Kelp is another name for seaweed, so it's sort of a joke meaning anyone who loves the water is a kelper. They have a crazy parade with cars covered in seaweed. A shake rat is a nickname for shake cutters—people who cut logs into smaller pieces. Part of the festival is the Shake Rat Olympics, where people show off their special skills. And there's even a kids' parade we can join.

 It is the latitude that separates the United States from Canada, from Minnesota to Washington. The Oregon Treaty of 1846 made it an international border.

Look at those mountains—they're all white, and it's not even winter.

You're looking at the Olympic Mountains; that's how this city got its name. Of course, before the settlers came, Native Americans had lived in this territory for thousands of years. They even spoke a language of their own, called Lushootseed.

Lushootseed?! I can't even say the name of the language.

I know. But it was really helpful, because all these different tribes—the Squaxin, Nisqually, Puyallup, Chehalis, Suquamish, and Duwamish—could communicate by speaking the same tongue. It was 1792 by the time Europeans came to this part of the country, when Peter Puget and his expedition started mapping the surrounding land. Our whole state is very young compared with much of the country. Believe it or not, the state capitol building in Olympia was a log cabin until 1903!

Q. What's so special about one Dairy Queen in Olympia?

Wow, that sounds like pioneer living!

Well, most people who came to America came from Europe and settled close to where they landed on the East Coast. We Washingtonians have the really brave pioneers and frontiersmen to thank who made their way west to start out on their own.

Pioneers like George Washington Bush and Peter Puget?

Correct! Olympia is at the very southern tip of Puget Sound, which is, by the way, an arm of the Pacific Ocean. And there's plenty of fun to be had in Olympia nowadays. In August, the city becomes a beach! They cart in 240 tons of sand, and everybody shows up and makes sand sculptures. It's called Sand in the City, and it lasts for four days. But now we should visit the Olympia Flight Museum. There are more than twenty planes and helicopters to see, lots of them dating back to World War II. They put on an awesome air show once a year too.

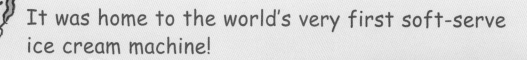

A. It was home to the world's very first soft-serve ice cream machine!

13

Sounds like the Native Americans have been here forever. When did explorers and settlers first arrive?

Spain had a claim on lots of land, including the entire coast of North America, through a treaty signed in 1494. No one in Spain paid this part of the world much attention, though, until they heard that both the Russians and the British were sniffing around the area. So, in 1775, Don Bruno de Heceta sailed north from Mexico on the Santiago and reclaimed the Pacific Northwest for Spain.

Why did everyone want to claim this part of the world for their country?

Well, they saw the same things then that make this land so valuable today: salmon fishing, lumber, valuable ports, and beautiful land rich with food. But what they had their eyes on most back then was the sea otter.

Why? What was so great about the sea otter?

It was the fur. Remember, this part of the world gets pretty cold, and animal fur in the eighteenth century was used to clothe people. There were plenty of sea otters, so that's

Q. Where did the saying "low man on the totem pole" come from?

how the fur-trading business got started here. Soon fur-trading posts began to spring up. Before you knew it, there were cities and towns too. Still, it was a long time before Washington became a state. First it was part of a larger area called the Washington Territory, but in 1889, it became the forty-second state of the United States.

Where are we now? I thought Vancouver was in Canada.

It is, but it's here in Washington too. That's because General George Vancouver of the British Navy did lots of exploration around these parts. Hudson's Bay Company established Fort Vancouver in 1825. It was their fur-trading headquarters out West, and the base of everything cultural and political too. So when pioneers started to come here to farm beginning in the 1840s, Fort Vancouver was their destination.

Wait a minute. Is that a totem pole?

It sure is. Totem means "kinship group" in Ojibwe, a Native American language. The Native Americans used totems to honor someone— either dead or alive—or to tell stories. The biggest one in Washington is 140 feet high and is in Kalama. Totems are usually made of Western red cedar. You won't see many totem poles left from before 1800 because, like regular trees, they decay.

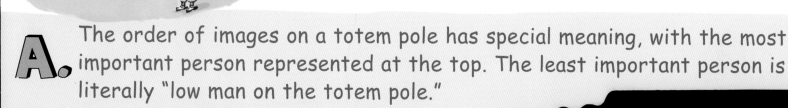

A. The order of images on a totem pole has special meaning, with the most important person represented at the top. The least important person is literally "low man on the totem pole."

What city is this?

It's Tacoma, the city halfway between Olympia and Seattle. It's also at the southern end of Puget Sound. In fact, some people call this area "Pugetopolis."

That sounds like a dinosaur.

There's a great zoo and aquarium here and a special museum called the Karpeles Manuscript Library. This place has unbelievable stuff, including the first draft of the Bill of Rights, Albert Einstein's description of his theory of relativity, Webster's Dictionary, and lots of other stuff.

Tacoma is called the City of Destiny because it was the end of the Northern Pacific Railroad back in the 1800s. The railroad ended near the water, so cargo brought here to the Pacific Northwest could then be put on boats and shipped to other places. Tacoma's motto became "When rails meet sails."

There were lots of travelers in the Pacific Northwest at the end of the nineteenth century. People heard there was gold in Alaska—this is long before Alaska was a state—and

16

Q. Who was Fay Fuller?

they would pack up and move, just on a rumor; these people were called prospectors. During the Klondike Gold Rush, cities like Portland, Oregon, Tacoma, and Seattle saw lots of folks passing through, but not all of them stayed and settled down.

For thousands of years, the Puyallup Indians lived in this area. In fact, there's a huge state fair called the Puyallup Fair here every year, and more than a million people come!

Wait a minute. Is that gigantic egg part of the fair?

Nope. A town called Winlock used to be the second biggest egg producer in the country, and in 1923 someone made the egg when the new Pacific Highway was coming through, as a symbol of pride. The egg is twelve feet long and weighs 1,200 pounds. The sign underneath says "World's Largest EGG, Winlock."

 Fay was a schoolteacher in Tacoma who became the first woman to climb Mount Rainier, in 1890.

I thought you said we were going to a park!

This *is* a park—Mount Rainier State Park. You're looking at Mount Rainier: At 14,410 feet, it's the tallest peak in the Cascade Volcanic Arc. It also has the most glaciers: twenty-six. One of them is called the Nisqually, and it's the fastest-moving glacier in the country; it moves sixteen inches a day during the summer! Believe it or not, more than 10,000 people each year climb Mount Rainier. It's really difficult to do; it takes two or three days. And no wonder—the National Park Service says that Paradise, an area on the south side of Mount Rainier, is the snowiest place in the world—that is, of the places where snow is regularly measured. Paradise is the most popular place in the entire park, partly because of the old Paradise Inn, where lots of hikers like to stay. There's also a tree house that's fifty feet up in a red cedar tree, and you can stay overnight in it—just like a monkey!

Q. Who was Mount St. Helens named after?

Is Mount Rainier the volcano that erupted?

Nope, Mount Rainier is an inactive volcano. It's Mount St. Helens that caused all the trouble, back in 1980. It was the deadliest volcano eruption in U.S. history, and it destroyed people's homes, bridges, train tracks, and highways. It even caused an avalanche so huge that the mountain went from 9,677 feet to 8,365 feet high, and it left a huge, horseshoe-shaped crater. There was so much volcanic ash that for miles around it was dark, even during the daytime.

Was that the first time it happened?

No. We know Mount St. Helens erupted at least once before in the nineteenth century. And scientists have discovered that ancient civilizations lived near here because they've found remains of their towns. They lived here more than 3,000 years ago.

A. General George Vancouver named the volcano for his friend, British Diplomat Lord St. Helens, who never actually saw the mountain!

Now we're going to a park on the Olympic Peninsula that's bigger than that whole state of Rhode Island!

Really? That's incredible!

Olympic National Park is more 1,400 square miles, and it has every kind of terrain you can imagine. The park can be divided up into three sections: there's the coast, which is on the Pacific; the Olympic Mountains, of course; and the best part of all, a rainforest!

I thought rainforests were only in places like South America.

This is different; it's not a tropical rainforest—it's a temperate rainforest. You'll see all kinds of interesting things there, but let's go to the beach first.

Q. How did the Olympic Mountains get their name?

What's wrong with the water? No one is swimming!

The beaches are beautiful here, but very rugged. The water is cold too, but park visitors can backpack along the beach; the coastline is so long you can hike all day. We're at sea level, the lowest point in Washington, and on our way to one of the highest points: Mount Olympus. In fact, we'll pass by the tallest tree in the state—a Douglas fir tree that's 298 feet tall!

The rainforest is my favorite part of the park. It's the wettest part of the continental United States—only the island of Kaui in Hawaii gets more rain. The rainforest here is filled with timber and some totally wild animals, like cougars, mountain lions, deer, elk, and puma.

Yikes! Isn't there anything less scary?

Oh sure, there's woodpeckers, owls—even flying squirrels! Let's go on a tour with a ranger and learn more about the wildflowers, Native American art, geology, and other fun things to see here.

It sure is beautiful—I've never seen anything like it! Being here is like being in all different places in the world all at once!

 Captain John Mearse, an English navigator, named them in 1788. They reminded him of Greece's Mount Olympus, a place beautiful enough for the mythical Greek gods to live on.

George, look out there at all those beautiful boats. Do you think it's a race?

It's the Wooden Boat Festival here in Port Townsend. Every year hundreds of boats come here for a regatta—that's a boat race. They're all different kinds of boats, but they have to be made of wood. There are boatbuilding classes, music, and even a pirate treasure hunt for kids.

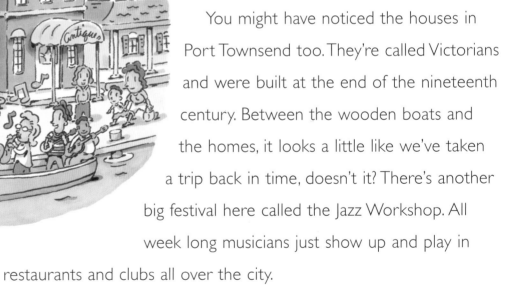

You might have noticed the houses in Port Townsend too. They're called Victorians and were built at the end of the nineteenth century. Between the wooden boats and the homes, it looks a little like we've taken a trip back in time, doesn't it? There's another big festival here called the Jazz Workshop. All week long musicians just show up and play in restaurants and clubs all over the city.

Q. What does Washington have more of per person than any other state?

OK, Mimi, now here's a scary question: have you ever heard of Bigfoot?

Sure, but I don't believe he's real—do you?

Everybody knows about Bigfoot in this part of the world. In Canada they call him Sasquatch, which is Native American language for "hairy giant." In Tibet, they call him Yeti—or you might have heard him called the Abominable Snowman too. I totally believe in him.

Different tribes all over Washington have sworn for hundreds of years they've seen Bigfoot. He is supposed to have feet as big as a person's size 28 shoe, weigh maybe nine hundred pounds, and measure eight feet tall. Some folks say he has only four toes! Lots of scientists say there's no Bigfoot because they've never found old bones. They think people just pull pranks, but there are plenty of reports of Native Americans seeing Bigfoot as many as 150 years ago!

 A. Coffee bean roasters! Washington is considered the coffee capital of the United States.

Welcome to Seattle, which was first called New York!

What?! Wasn't there already a New York on the East Coast!

There was, but Seattle was first called New York too, and then it was called Duwamps, after a local tribe, and finally Seattle, after an Indian chief named Chief Noah Sealth. The first settlers in Seattle were a group of pioneers led by Arthur A. Denny, back in 1851. We're talking about European explorers and settlers, of course. The Duwamish Indians had nearly twenty villages scattered around what is now Seattle when Denny arrived.

Now Seattle is the biggest city in all of the Pacific Northwest, with more than 600,000 people. It's called the Emerald City because of all the evergreen trees.

Q. **What else about Washington is Olympic (besides the park)?**

Wow! Well, it sure looks busy now. How did it become so big?

First there was a lot of lumber business, and then the Klondike Gold Rush came along. Seattle's right on Puget Sound, so getting cargo, supplies, and people in and out is easy. Shipbuilding became big in Seattle too, and during World War II, lots of ships left here to fight in the Pacific. Warplanes were also built in Seattle. Then when commercial aviation took off, the Boeing Company, which was located here, was key.

I heard it rains here all the time, but it hasn't so far.

I know—it is a total myth! In fact, it rains here less than it does in New York City. But it is often cloudy; on average nearly 250 days a year are overcast. But it doesn't get that cold; you hardly ever see snow in Seattle.

What else can we do in Seattle?

There's a big music scene in Seattle. Grunge music, which was really big in the 1990s, originated here. And maybe the greatest guitarist of all time, Jimi Hendrix, was born here. We can learn all about him at the Experience Music Project. There's great stuff like videos of musicians telling their stories, a whole gallery of guitars—and part of the building is also the Science Fiction Museum and Hall of Fame. It's a really wild place.

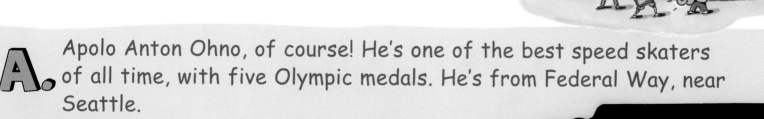

A. Apolo Anton Ohno, of course! He's one of the best speed skaters of all time, with five Olympic medals. He's from Federal Way, near Seattle.

25

Riding those ferries looks like loads of fun.

Can you believe that Seattle has the biggest fleet of ferries in the country? There were many boats here even one hundred years ago, when they were called the Mosquito Fleet—little steamers carrying travelers all over Puget Sound. There are nearly thirty ferries now—some can carry 2,500 passengers and more than two hundred cars. They travel all around Seattle, to the San Juan Islands and into Canada.

So many people are reading: on the ferries, in the parks, and coffeehouses—everywhere!

It's funny you noticed. Seattle not only has more college graduates than any other city in the United States, but it's also known to be the most literate city.

So people are really smart here?

Well, some of them have been really successful, that's for sure. You've heard of Amazon.com. It was started right here in Seattle. It was one of the first companies to sell things over the Internet.

26

Q. What is the Pike Place Market?

Starbucks started here too, in 1971. It's named Starbucks after the first mate in the book, *Moby-Dick*.

But Seattle's biggest claim to fame might be Microsoft, the software company. It's located in Redmond, right outside Seattle, and employs more than 30,000 people. Bill Gates—he founded the company—is not just a billionaire: he's the second richest person in the whole world!

One more thing before we go: what's that crazy pointy building in the middle of the city?

That's the Space Needle from the 1962 Seattle World's Fair. You can still go to the top and have dinner. It was the first revolving restaurant in the world. It makes a complete revolution in forty-seven minutes. It goes slowly so you won't have to worry about getting dizzy!

 It's the longest continuously operating farmers' market in the United States. It opened in 1907 and is Seattle's most popular tourist spot.

Let's zip up to the town of Anacortes, at the top of Puget Sound on Fidalgo Island. Anacortes sounds kind of French, but actually it's a misspelling of somebody's name: Annie Curtis, who was the wife of an early settler here. Lots of ferries to all the San Juan Islands take off from Anacortes.

I thought San Juan was a city in Puerto Rico.

It's also the name given to these islands by a Spanish explorer, Francisco de Eliza, back in 1791, when he was charting them. There are 450 islands, but most of them don't even have people; you can only get to six of the islands by ferry. Tourism is also a huge industry in Washington, and

these islands are *the* place to visit for out-of-towners. Some of the small islands have crazy names, like Deadman Island, Skull Island, and Cemetery Island.

Q. What national holiday began in Washington?

This map says there's a Strawberry Island too. That's the place for me! What's fun to do here?

Here and all over the San Juan Islands there are tons of sports to try: boating, orca watching, bird watching, hiking, scuba diving, and sea kayaking, which is a lot rougher than just paddling around on a lake—it's pretty extreme. It's almost like surfing in a boat! We can ski here too!

Ski?!

There's a great team relay race that ends in a town called Bellingham that's got seven different sports in it: they call it the Ski to Sea Race, and people come from all over to compete. They begin at the Mount Baker Ski Area and finish on Bellingham Bay, and it includes cross-country skiing, downhill skiing or snowboarding, running, biking, canoeing, mountain biking, and kayaking. Mount Baker even claims a world record for seasonal snowfall: in the 1998 to 1999 season, it snowed 1,140 inches!

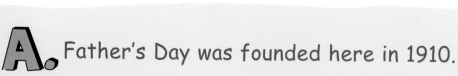

A. Father's Day was founded here in 1910.

What's going on here? It seems like loads of fun.

This is the Seafair Festival. It started in 1950, and it's grown to be a huge festival. There are hydroplane races and a milk-carton derby, where people make their boats out of empty milk cartons. There's a nighttime torchlight parade with illuminated floats, foot races, and the navy even sails ships into the Puget Sound so you can go on board. Seafair is so famous that two presidents, Richard M. Nixon and John F. Kennedy, have enjoyed the festivities.

I love all the activities we can do on water. I hope you haven't forgotten that you promised to take us whale watching.

S.S. Got Milk

That's next on our list! We'll see the orca, or killer whale, which is the official state mammal. It's technically in the dolphin family, but because of its size, most people consider the orca to be

S.S. Whale Watcher

30

Q. What popular games originated in Washington?

a whale. They're not endangered, but people are not allowed to hunt them either. Whales will come right up to the boat—they're very sociable. But the orca is only interested in eating fish and other large animals and mammals, like sea lions, seal, and even other whales.

But speaking of eating, let's try Washington's famous salmon!

My teacher told us something strange about salmon.

It's wild! Salmon do this mysterious thing every year where they swim hundreds of miles upstream, against the current, to lay their eggs; it's called spawning. And even though they're born in fresh water, many of them go out to sea and live in the salt water. Scientists say it's one of the most amazing feats of the entire animal kingdom.

Whew

A. Pictionary, Pickle-ball, and Cranium were all invented in the state.

Now we're in Everett, which is just north of Seattle, and it's also on the water.

It seems like the rivers and ocean have always been important for everybody around here, from the Native Americans to the fish!

You're right. The navy built Naval Station Everett here in 1992, and now it is homeport to the USS *Abraham Lincoln*.

Is there anything else that's famous in Everett?

As a matter of fact there is—the Boeing assembly plant. They make the 747, 767, 777, and 787 planes here in the largest building, by volume, in the entire world! It's a bona fide Guinness World Record holder!

No way!

Q. What is Washingtonian Chester Carlson famous for?

Yup. The building is 472,000,000 cubic feet and more than ninety acres. The planes look like toys inside such a big space. And here's something cool: at the Boeing plant, there's a railroad turntable built in 1899 by the Great Northern Railroad. So railcars come right into the factory for unloading. We can take a tour of the plant and watch the planes being built.

What else can we do in Everett?

From the largest to the smallest, welcome to the Wayside Chapel, the world's smallest church, right outside of Everett in Sultan. *This* building is only seven by nine feet; there's room for eight people and a pulpit.

And there's one more thing you should know about this area: the famous artist Chuck Close was born in Monroe. He became a quadriplegic, so he started painting by holding a paintbrush in his teeth. His paintings are made of thousands of tiny, differently painted squares; but when you stand back, it looks like a normal painting. It's amazing!

A. He invented the process of instant copying, in 1937, which was originally called electrophotography. It was renamed Xerography from the Greek for "dry writing."

Let's go apple picking!

Almost twelve billion apples are picked each year in Washington, and they're all picked by hand! Red Delicious seems to be everyone's favorite apple, though there are almost 250 varieties here. During the apple-picking season, which is August to November, almost 40,000 people help pick apples.

I know Washington has more than just high-tech stuff.
I've seen lots of farms.

You're right. Washington also grows 90 percent of the red raspberries in the country. We also grow hops, which are used to make beer, spearmint oil, sweet cherries, pears, and Concord and Niagara grapes, which are funny names since neither Concord nor Niagara are locations in this state. We also produce a lot of wheat.

 Who was William O. Douglas?

Agriculture is a huge part of Washington's economy. Even though the apple is the major state food here, the steelhead trout, which is actually a kind of salmon, is often named as another state food, along with Dungeness crabs.

So people in Washington might've made or grown some of the food we ate for dinner last night?

That's right. With the other important industries here like fishing and salmon canning, Washington produces food for millions of people.

Washington is also known for its lumber. We cut loads of lumber and make lots of wood products from books to houses to labels on soup cans.

How do they move all those large trees for lumber?

Have you ever been on a log flume ride in an amusement park? Well, log flumes really existed to transport lumber down the mountains to the railroads. A really famous one, the Broughton Log Flume, was constructed of fir and cedar, and the water, which came from the Little White Salmon River, flowed at nine miles an hour, helping to bring the cut timber down the mountain.

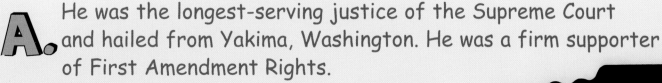

A. He was the longest-serving justice of the Supreme Court and hailed from Yakima, Washington. He was a firm supporter of First Amendment Rights.

I figured you might want some cider, what with all the talk of apples, so let's stop at the Marcus Cider Festival. More than one thousand people come to see this crazy cider press and enjoy the pancakes, a parade, arts and crafts, and music. We're close to Wenatchee, which calls itself the Apple Capital of the World. It's also home to the Wenatchee Youth Circus, which is entirely performed by kids—some of them as young as three years old! They do everything a regular circus does, and they travel all over the place.

Hey, George, look at that sign: "Kettle Falls—1,550 Friendly People and One Grouch." I wonder who the grouch is?

I've heard about this place! Every year, everybody pays a quarter a vote to pick the crabbiest person in town. You can vote as many times as you want— even kids get to vote!

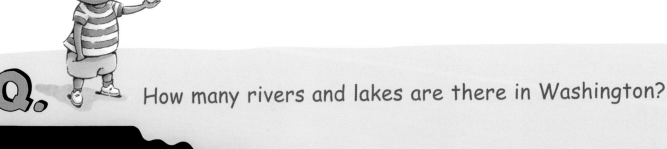

Q. How many rivers and lakes are there in Washington?

These little towns sure are fun, but now I'm going to show you something really, really big.

Yipes! Where are we? This is humongous!

Here we are at the Grand Coulee Dam.

During the Great Depression in the 1930s, President Franklin D. Roosevelt kept lots of people working through a program called the WPA, or Works Progress Administration. The Grand Coulee Dam started as one of these projects; it was one of a series of hydroelectric dams built to increase production of electricity. Now, three-quarters of Washington gets electricity from this dam.

How big is it?

It's the largest electric power–producing center and the biggest concrete structure in the entire country. It's almost a mile long and taller than the Great Pyramid of Giza in Egypt. It's twice as tall as Niagara Falls!

 A. The state has more than 40,000 miles of rivers and streams and more than 8,000 lakes!

Is this Spokane? The weather feels so different here.

That's because we're on the other side of the Cascades, and it's much drier. Spokane is the second-largest city in Washington and just a few miles from the Idaho state line. It got its name from the Spokan tribe, which means "Children of the Sun."

It's also known as the Lilac City—there's even a Lilac Festival! It's every spring, when the lilacs come out; then you know summer vacation isn't far behind, and then we can ride on the carousel.

Is that it over there? You weren't horsing around!

Charles Looff built this carousel in Riverside Park in 1909. It's one of the most beautiful and famous carousels in the country. I'll bet you noticed the other awesome thing in this park:

Q. What was once the smallest city to host a World's Fair?

Spokane Falls, the second biggest urban waterfall in the country. And there's one more thing that means summer in Spokane: Hoopfest!

Is that a basketball party?

The best basketball event ever! It's all three-on-three play, and when it started it had just three hundred teams. Now people of all ages play on four hundred different courts all over Spokane. We love basketball in Washington: both the Seattle Supersonics and the woman's team, the Seattle Storm, have brought championships home.

Tell me more about the Spokan Indians.

They originally settled around the Spokane River because it had lots of salmon. In 1871, two settlers named James J. Downing and Seth Scranton built a sawmill here, and eventually a man named James N. Glover bought the sawmill, built a bank, and became the founding father of the new city of Spokane.

Why are there so many forts all over?

Well, there were battles all over the United States during its growth west, which were called the Indian Wars. Remember, the Native Americans had lived here thousands of years, and now the new settlers were fishing in their rivers, killing their buffalo, and taking their land.

A. Up until 1982, Spokane was the smallest city to host the fair. Some fair attractions like the carousel and Washington State Pavilion are still around today.

We're on the last leg of our tour now. But there are still a few more places I want to show you: the first one is Walla Walla.

The home of the onion!

You're right! The Walla Walla sweet onion is the state vegetable of Washington. There's even a Walla Walla Sweet Onion Festival. People here like to say Walla Walla is "the town so nice they named it twice!"

Walla Walla has sort of an odd history, because there were always big plans that didn't work out. First there were Narcissa and Marcus Whitman, who started the unsuccessful Whitman mission in the 1830s to convert the Walla Walla Indians. The Walla Wallas killed them after a deadly epidemic of measles spread around the tribe.

Q. What great superhero hails from Walla Walla?

Then the gold rush made Walla Walla the biggest city in the territory for a while, so they built a state capitol building and a governor's mansion here. But then Olympia was made the capital instead! The governor's mansion is still standing today; it's too bad the governor didn't get to live in it.

One really neat thing out here is the Walla Walla Fair and Frontier Days. They've been hosting it every summer since 1886, soon after people started settling here. There's a night rodeo, a demolition derby, concerts, horse racing, and tons of food.

Yippee-ki-yo!

Lots of people come out this way because there are more than one hundred wineries nearby, and you can go on tours and see the grapes on the vine. Just seeing how wine gets made is fun too—it's like a giant chemistry set!

A. Adam West, the original TV Batman, is from here.

You know, all this time, I've been waiting for you to tell me about Lewis and Clark.

Well, where we are now is pretty much the route Lewis and Clark traveled when the expedition entered what's now the state of Washington on October 10, 1805. By November 20, Lewis and Clark saw the Pacific Ocean, having followed the Columbia River all the way to its mouth.

Meriweather Lewis and William Clark were handpicked by President Thomas Jefferson to make the trip. In fact, Lewis was Jefferson's personal secretary. He started out on August 31, 1803, from Pittsburgh, Pennsylvania, and met up with Clark in Indiana. They had specific instructions from the president: to map out a new route to the Pacific, make contact with Native Americans, observe or collect animal and plant specimens, and keep a record of all their activities.

It sounds like an expensive trip.

It cost $2,500 for all forty-two people in the Corps of Discovery—plus Seaman, Lewis's black Newfoundland dog!

Q. Who is Gary Locke?

Lewis & Clark
To Do LIST
1. Find Pacific! ✓
2. Find River Route through Rockies. ✓
3. Map Everything. ✓
4. Contact Native Americans. ✓
5. Keep a journal. ✓
6. Collect specimans of plants & animals. ✓
7. Don't get lost! ✓
INK

Did they do everything they were supposed to?

Yes, and they kept detailed diaries that you can still read today about their adventures. They found all sorts of stuff no one had ever seen back East—more than 178 plants and 122 species and subspecies of animals, like the prairie dog, porcupine, grizzly bear, black-billed magpie, bald eagle, western rattlesnake, and Ponderosa pine, just to name a few. They were the first team in the United States to make an overland expedition to the Pacific and back.

What about Sacagawea?

She was the Shoshone heroine! When she was a girl in Idaho, she was kidnapped and brought up in North Dakota. She married a white man named Charbonneau and was pregnant when Lewis and Clark discovered her and asked her to be their translator. She accompanied the expedition with her tiny baby in tow. On more than one occasion Sacagawea saved the day—she was really brave. Now there's a one-dollar piece with her likeness on it.

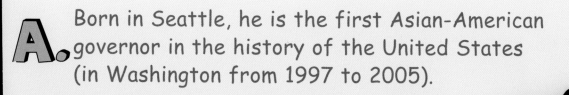

A. Born in Seattle, he is the first Asian-American governor in the history of the United States (in Washington from 1997 to 2005).

What's that up ahead?
It looks familiar!

You're right, Mimi. You're looking at a full-size, exact replica of Stonehenge, overlooking the Columbia River in Maryhill. A man named Sam Hill, a road builder, constructed it to memorialize all those who died in World War I. It took from the end of the war in 1918 until 1930 to build it, and Mr. Hill is buried at the base. We call it Little Stonehenge.

While we're here we can also visit the Maryhill Museum of Art. It's in a building that looks just like a medieval castle!

Q. What does "Alki" mean?

Sam Hill built his home to look like a castle and situated it on a bluff overlooking the Columbia River. Maryhill is named for his daughter, Mary. After his death the mansion was turned into a museum, and now people today can visit this beautiful spot to appreciate nature and fine art.

I can hardly believe how brave people were back then, George. Your ancestors, Lewis and Clark, and all the men and women who came out here to explore and settle on new land.

"Westward ho!" is what they used to say. It seems like nothing could stop them. And, remember, they built the railroads too: both the Great Northern and Northern Pacific Railroads came cross country in the nineteenth century, joining East and West for the first time. Finally it was possible to travel from one end of our great country to the other.

It's a great place to end your story, George. Lily and I have loved every minute. Thank you so much—we'll be back real soon!

A. It's the state motto and is Chinook for "Bye and bye," as in, "I'll be seeing you bye and bye."

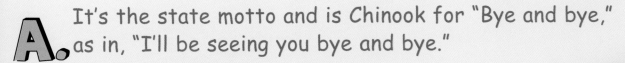